The Need To Hold Still

Also by Lisel Mueller

Dependencies
The Private Life

The Need
To Hold Still
Poems by Lisel Mueller

Louisiana State University Press
Baton Rouge and London 1980

Design: Patricia Douglas Crowder
Typeface: VIP Trump
Typesetter: LSU Press

Acknowledgment is made to the following publications in which
some of these poems first appeared: *Ark River Review, Chicago Re-
view, Chowder Review, Missouri Review, Mother Jones, New England
Review, Poetry Northwest, Southern Review, Virginia Quarterly
Review.*

"Merce Cunningham and the Birds" appeared originally in *The New
Yorker.*

"Night Song," "Drawings by Children," "The End of Science Fiction,"
and "Fiction" appeared originally in the *Ohio Review.*

"The Artist's Model, ca. 1912," "Why We Tell Stories," "The Story,"
and "Found in the Cabbage Patch" appeared originally in *Poetry.*

"Voices from the Forest," "Sometimes, When the Light," "Daughter,"
and "Another Version" first appeared in the chapbook *Voices from the
Forest*. Special thanks to John Judson, publisher of Juniper Press, La
Crosse, Wisconsin.

Two of these poems were also included in anthologies: "The End of
Science Fiction" in *The Pushcart Prize II: Best of the Small Presses,*
and "A Voice from out of the Night" in *A Geography of Poets.*

LIBRARY OF CONGRESS CATALOGING IN PUBLICATION DATA

Mueller, Lisel.
    The need to hold still.

    I. Title.
PS3563.U35N4   811'.5'4   79–20965
ISBN 0–8071–0669–0
ISBN 0–8071–0670–4 pbk.

In memory of my father and mother, Fritz and Ilse Neumann

"So, the world happens twice—
once what we see it as;
second it legends itself
deep, the way it is." WILLIAM STAFFORD

Contents

I

For a Thirteenth Birthday

You have read *War and Peace*.
Now here is *Sister Carrie*,
not up to Tolstoy; still
it will second the real world:
predictable planes and levels,
pavement that holds you,
stairs that lift you,
ice that trips you,
nights that begin after sunset,
four lunar phases,
a finite house.

I give you Dreiser
although (or because)
I am no longer sure.
Lately I have been walking into glass doors.
Through the car windows, curbs disappear.
On the highway, wrong turnoffs become irresistible,
someone else is controlling the wheel.
Sleepless nights pile up like a police record;
all my friends are getting divorced.
Language, my old comrade, deserts me;
words are misused or forgotten,
consonants fight each other
between my upper and lower teeth.
I write "fiend" for "friend"
and "word" for "world",
remember comes out with an "m" missing.

I used to be able to find my way in the dark,
sure of the furniture,
but the town I lived in for years
has pulled up its streets in my absence,
disguised its buildings behind my back.
My neighbor at dinner glances
at his cuffs, his palms;
he has memorized certain phrases,
but does not speak my language.
Suddenly I am aware
no one at the table does.

4   And so I give you Dreiser,
     his measure of certainty:
     a table that's oak all the way through,
     real and fragrant flowers,
     skirts from sheep and silkworms,
     no unknown fibers;
     a language as plain as money,
     a workable means of exchange;
     a world whose very meanness is solid,
     mud into mortar, and you are sure
     of what will injure you.

     I give you names like nails,
     walls that withstand your pounding,
     doors that are hard to open,
     but once they are open, admit you
     into rooms that breathe pure sun.
     I give you trees that lose their leaves,
     as you knew they would,
     and then come green again.
     I give you
     fruit preceded by flowers,
     Venus supreme in the sky,
     the miracle of always
     landing on your feet,
     even though the earth
     rotates on its axis.

     Start out with that, at least.

Another Version

Our trees are aspens, but people
mistake them for birches;
they think of us as characters
in a Russian novel, Kitty and Levin
living contentedly in the country.
Our friends from the city watch the birds
and rabbits feeding together
on top of the deep, white snow.
(We have Russian winters in Illinois,
but no sleighbells, possums instead of wolves,
no trusted servants to do our work.)
As in a Russian play, an old man
lives in our house, he is my father;
he lets go of life in such slow motion,
year after year, that the grief
is stuck inside me, a poisoned apple
that won't go up or down.
But like the three sisters, we rarely speak
of what keeps us awake at night;
like them, we complain about things
that don't really matter and talk
of our pleasures and of the future:
we tell each other the willows
are early this year, hazy with green.

The Middle Distance

6   You have retreated behind your eyes
    to enter your other life,
    the real one, where you are
    in charge of the characters

    Your childhood has been corrected
    and you are not going to die
    and you keep moving toward a figure
    whose arms stretch out to you

    It is always the same figure
    and the distance remains the same

Drawings by Children

1

The sun may be visible or not
(it may be behind you,
the viewer of these pictures)
but the sky is always blue
if it is day. If not,
the stars come almost within your grasp;
crooked, they reach out to you,
on the verge of falling.
It is never sunrise or sunset;
there is no bloody eye
spying on you across the horizon.
It is clearly day or night,
it is bright or totally dark,
it is here and never there.

2

In the beginning, you only needed
your head, a moon swimming in space,
and four bare branches;
and when your body was added,
it was light and thin at first,
not yet the dark chapel
from which, later, you tried to escape.
You lived in a non-Newtonian world,
your arms grew up from your shoulders,
your feet did not touch the ground,
your hair was streaming,
you were still flying.

8   3
The house is smaller than you remembered,
it has windows but no door.
A chimney sits on the gable roof,
a curl of smoke reassures you.
But the house has only two dimensions,
like a mask without its face;
the people who live there stand outside
as though time were always summer—
there is nothing behind the wall
except a space where the wind whistles,
but you cannot see that.

Fiction

Going south, we watched spring
unroll like a proper novel:
forsythia, dogwood, rose;
bare trees, green lace, full shade.
By the time we arrived in Georgia
the complications were deep.

When we drove back, we read
from back to front. Maroon went wild,
went scarlet, burned once more
and then withdrew into pink,
tentative, still in bud.
I thought if only we could go on
and meet again, shy as strangers.

Sometimes, When the Light

Sometimes, when the light strikes at odd angles
and pulls you back into childhood

and you are passing a crumbling mansion
completely hidden behind old willows

or an empty convent guarded by hemlocks
and giant firs standing hip to hip,

you know again that behind that wall,
under the uncut hair of the willows

something secret is going on,
so marvelous and dangerous

that if you crawled through and saw,
you would die, or be happy forever.

Poppy

When they stop reaching for the moon,
the children begin to reach for the poppy.
They know without knowing that death is red,
its petals thinner than the thin skin
of their crackling crepe paper fevers,
and that it has a dark center
in which they can disappear.

It is not that they want to die,
only to come as close to death
as anyone has who is still alive,
run through the fire quickly enough,
pull open the parachute just in time.
They want to taste one pollen grain
from the bitter bread that grows
among the yellow, ignorant wheat.
Years later they will reveal to you
there was a time when they almost drowned
in the river that flows backwards,
the water that has no place to go.
They will tell you as gently as they can.

Postcards from All Over

12 Nefertiti's head
and Mozart's piano float to the top
side by side, like contemporaries;
briefly, the long, diagonal neck
is a possible answer
to the piano legs,
rococo, short and curved.

Then Matisse's altar cloth
lowers doves and seaweed
over the empty face
of a Florida swimming pool.

The Third of May arrived from Madrid;
the shirt of the man before
the firing squad is unbearably white.

Someone thought of us in Madrid,
and someone else in the Andes,
and in Heiligenstadt,
where Beethoven almost gave up.

I look for a long time
at the ancient limestone couple
united by the burial feast;
she sits astride his thighs,
his whole body is smiling.
I am in the museum of love and death.

A friend wrote, "Here is the well
where she discovered language."
Another sent me *greetings*
at the time of happiness.
The picture is of a place
where he has never been.

Talking to Helen
Helen Keller, 1880–1968

1. The Source

A well
that ran deeper
than roots
and memory

a spring
that wanted to climb
into a world
of mirrors

a pump and a hand
that spoke
the thing and its name

the flash
so cold, so clear
it burned like ice
before
it bloomed
into light

2. The Word *Water*

The word *water*, meaning

what leaps on your hands
under the pump

what crawls down your back
from the washcloth

what runs down your cheeks
and tastes salty

what licks your feet
in the early morning grass

what spits out smooth rocks
and lets you fly like a fish

what coaxes green
from black and brown seeds
(Helen, try to imagine green!)

what has one home in the sky,
another in the earth

what will teach you
the word *deep*
and the word *cleanse*

the word *flow*
and the word *drown*

the word *inexhaustible*
and the word *birth*

what is beginning to quench your thirst
for the real name of the world

3. The Saviors

Before you knew the word *dream*
and the word *fire*, you dreamed of fires.
Later you wrote how the swaying shapes
—orange, were they, did you
dream in color?—
closed in around you, hot
and threatening, a lynch mob
from which you could not escape
except by screaming and waking.
Then the words came,
kept coming: *water, mother,*
father, flower, door,
earth, give, open,
a growing army, proof
against the ring of fire.
You slept. You smiled in your sleep.
You slept all night without screaming.
You still did not know the word
language, the word *saved*.

4. The Word *Feeling*

"You feel with your fingers,"
the teacher told us,

14

dismissing expressions
of love and fear.
He was a tyrant
and wore a large ring.

Years later, I understood,
when I read about you, at twelve,
in a Niagara Falls hotel,
your face overwhelmed
by the roar you felt
when you pressed your fingers
against the window sill,

and how, on another day,
you said you loved white roses,
meaning the thin-skinned sisters
of the fleshier reds.

5. The Word *Vast*

Flying above the clouds
I am in a blank space,
perhaps a sunlit version
of your darker world.

And breaking through the clouds
I am above a country
scaled to your palpable map,
your raised geography.

I dream of touching the winter trees,
their stiff unruly hair,
and the collection of roofs
from a child's bag of blocks;
the land laid out like a chocolate bar,
squares bordered by ridges
that intersect at right angles;
hills that fit in the palm of your hand,
railroad tracks for your fingers.

I used to wonder how you made
the leap from your shallow liquid
to the real Mississippi,
how you got to the ships that lie
on the Atlantic floor.

But coming down, approaching
—wheels out, already gripping
the runway—I think it was easy.
Your world was imagination,
all possible worlds, while mine
shrinks with the speed of speed.

One hour: New York/Chicago.
The long drawn-out idea
of the word *vast* contracts
into four brief letters,
already obsolete.

6. The Word *Autumn*

Helen, this is a maple leaf.
It is a hand. Put your fingers
against the five of the leaf
and feel how they match.
It is golden,
that is to say the feeling
that lies down deep inside you
like an unhurried animal
and keeps you warm longer
than green or red. Each tree
has a thousand golden hands,
soon they will fall around you.
Helen, it is autumn,
the sun today bears down
intense as an evangelist
and imprints each hand once more
with its large signature
before moving on to another town.

Daughter

My next poem will be happy,
I promise myself. Then you come
with your deep eyes, your tall jeans,
your narrow hands, your wit,
your uncanny knowledge and
your loneliness. All the flowers
your father planted, all
the green beans that have made it,
all the world's recorded pianos
and this exhilarating day
cannot change that.

This Sadness, This Happiness

18   This sadness, holding you
while your wings diminish;
my left hand traces
the cutting edge, safe now,
a shoulderblade. My other
walks the narrow street of your spine,
cobblestones, only room
for one. It is my street,
my fingers count each crack,
each irreplaceable bump,
five children spared the truth
in my head a little longer.

Beginning with 1914

Since it always begins
in the unlikeliest place,
we start in an obsolete country
on no current map. The camera
glides over flower beds,
for this is a southern climate.
We focus on medals, a horse,
on a white uniform,
for this is June. The young man
waves to the people lining the road,
he lifts a child, he catches
a rose from a wrinkled woman
in a blue kerchief. Then we hear shots
and close in on a casket
draped in the Austrian flag.
Thirty-one days torn off a calendar.
Bombs on Belgrade; then Europe explodes.
We watch the trenches fill with men,
the air with live ammunition.
A closeup of a five-year-old
living on turnips. Her older sister,
my not-yet-mother, already
wearing my daughter's eyes,
is reading a letter as we cut
to a young man with thick glasses
who lies in a trench and writes
a study of Ibsen. I recognize him,
he is going to be my father,
and this is his way of keeping alive.
Snow. Blood. Lice. Frostbite.
Grenades. Stretchers. Coffins. Snow.
Telegrams with black borders.
On the wide screen my father returns
bringing his brother's body;
my mother's father brings back his son's
from the opposite edge. They come together
under the oaks of the cemetery.
All who will be my family

20   are here, except my sister,
      who is not yet imagined.
      Neither am I, who imagine
      this picture, who now jump
      to my snowy birthday in the year
      of the million mark loaf of bread.
      My early years are played
      by a blue-eyed child who grows up
      quickly, for this is a film
      of highlights, like all documentaries
      false to the life; the work
      of selective memory, all I can bear
      of a painful childhood. The swastika
      appears and remains as the huge
      backdrop against which we're seen.
      The soundtrack of a hysterical voice
      is threatening us. We're heard as whispers.
      Shortly before my city
      bursts into flames, my stand-in
      disappears from the film, which continues
      with scenes of terror and death
      I can't bear to watch. I pick up
      a new reel, a strange sequel
      set in a different location
      and made in another language,
      in which I am back. The colors are bright,
      the soundtrack is filled with music,
      the focus gentle. A man is beside me.
      Time-lapse photography picks up
      the inchmeal growth of daughters
      toward the sky, the slow subversion
      of dark by gray hair. Little happens.
      The camera sums up the even flow
      of many years in a shot of a river.
      The principals from part one
      are missing, except for me
      who am the connection. The time is now,
      and I am playing myself.

II

Merce Cunningham and the Birds

Last night I saw Merce Cunningham and his ten amazing dancers
dancing for eighty minutes without a break in the college gym.

I am trying to tell you how it was
        but of course there are no words
        for being wholly enclosed in a space,
        a tight cocoon without chinks
        so none of the wonder will leak out

Instead, I ask you to watch the assorted birds
feeding outside this window,
darting and dropping and zeroing in,
assuming positions in groups of threes
        or fours, to break up and form
        new patterns, other groups

how each incessant performer
signals a personal flash of color:
cardinal red, jay blue,
towhee orange, March pea green
        of not-yet-yellow goldfinch,
always tempered with black

how even their silences prefigure
shifts already known to the muscles

        and how none leads or follows
        how each moves
        to the authority of its brain
        its autonomous body

        perpetual proof that the world

is energy, that to land
in a certain space at a certain time
is being alive; watch how they manage
to keep it up till each soul is fed

        and disappear into nowhere

Not Only the Eskimos

We have only one noun
but as many different kinds:

the grainy snow of the Puritans
and snow of soft, fat flakes,

guerrilla snow, which comes in the night
and changes the world by morning,

rabbinical snow, a permanent skullcap
on the highest mountains,

snow that blows in like the Lone Ranger,
riding hard from out of the West,

surreal snow in the Dakotas,
when you can't find your house, your street,
though you are not in a dream
or a science fiction movie,

snow that tastes good to the sun
when it licks black tree limbs,
leaving us only one white stripe,
a replica of a skunk,

unbelievable snows:
the blizzard that strikes on the 10th of April,
the false snow before Indian summer,
the Big Snow on Mozart's birthday,
when Chicago became the Elysian Fields
and strangers spoke to each other,

paper snow, cut and taped
to the inside of grade school windows,

in an old tale, the snow
that covers a nest of strawberries,
small hearts, ripe and sweet,

the special snow that goes with Christmas,
whether it falls or not,

the Russian snow we remember
along with the warmth and smell of our furs,
though we have never traveled
to Russia or worn furs,

Villon's snows of yesteryear,
lost with ladies gone out like matches,
the snow in Joyce's "The Dead,"
the silent, secret snow
in a story by Conrad Aiken,
which is the snow of first love,

the snowfall between the child
and the spacewoman on T. V.,

snow as idea of whiteness,
as in *snowdrop, snow goose, snowball bush,*

the snow that puts stars in your hair,
and your hair, which has turned to snow,

the snow Elinor Wylie walked in
in velvet shoes,

the snow before her footprints
and the snow after,

the snow in the back of our heads,
whiter than white, which has to do
with childhood again each year.

Eggs

26   Mothershape, how we love you!
In a dream we almost remember
the floating cushions, the waterbed;
in nightmares, we hack our way
out of the calcium walls
which refused to expand with us.

When we eat eggs, we return.
It's a matter of beginnings.
Heart attacks are forgotten
when the delicious, dangerous yellow
is rich and smooth as paint in the can
and the tasteless, foam-rubber white
transformed by a pinch of salt,

when we sit down for picnic lunches
and peel our way back inside,
the shell falling under our fingers
to reveal the gleaming rim,
the oval promise through which we come
to the holy of holies,
the green-tinged, golden, solid sphere,
a child's first model of the moon.

Found in the Cabbage Patch

The shiny head is round,
full term, between
the spread leaves of its mother.
I come as the midwife,
a kitchen knife in my hand.

There. No lusty cry,
this child is silent.
Two white moths
hover and flutter,
milky attendants
in perpetual motion.

I leave the mother's wound
for the sun to heal.
The stump of the newborn
dries in the crook of my arm.
I am the witch, cradling
the pale green head,
murmuring, "Little one,
you look good enough to eat."

One More Hymn to the Sun

28   You know that like an ideal mother
        she will never leave you,
        though after a week of rain
        you begin to worry

        but you accept her brief absences,
        her occasional closed doors
        as the prerogative
        of an eccentric lover

        You know which side of the bed
        she gets up on,
        though, being a night person,
        you are on more intimate terms
        with the moon, who lets you watch,
        while the sun will put out your eyes
        for tampering with her privacy

        She wants to be known by her parts,
        fingers, a flashing leg,
        a cheek, a shoulder; by things
        spilled from her purse:
        small change, a patterned scarf,
        mirrors, keys, an earring

        You like the fact that her moods
        are an orderly version of yours,
        arranged, like the needs of animals,
        by seasons: her spring quirks,
        her sexual summers,
        her steadfast warmth in the fall;
        you remember her face on Christmas Day,
        blurred, and suffused with the weak smile
        of a woman who has just given birth

        The way she loves you, your whole body,
        and still leaves enough space between you
        to keep you from turning to cinders
        before your time!

You admit she colors
everything you see,
that Renoir and Monet
are her direct descendants;
she could make you say
the grass is red, the snow purple

She never gave up on you
though it took you billions of years
to learn the alphabet
and the shadow you cast on the ground
changed its shape again and again

The Cook
After Vermeer

I

No wonder she thinks there's more
where everything came from

a girl as round as the jug
that never runs dry

her arms thick cream, her yellow bodice
filled with anticipation

the bread before her risen
in the same light in which she stands

2

She did not ask for this,
three centuries of tilting
a half-filled glazed brown jug
to show us the connection

the give and take, the earthen lip
feeding the earthen bowl

herself still bound to us
who watch the milk: it pours
and keeps on pouring,
although the paint is dry

Picking Raspberries

Once the thicket opens
and lets you enter
and the first berry dissolves on your tongue,

you will remember nothing
of your old life. You can stay
in that country of sun and silence
as long as you like. To return,

you have only to look at your arms
and discover the long, red marks.
You will have invented pain,
which has no place there.

Signs

32   They have entered the trees.
They let you know they are there
by a slight stir, an almost
imperceptible wave
in your direction as you pass;
by the current that runs through your cheek
when you place it against the bark,
and the ache when you sit for a long time
with your back against them—
a reminder of how it was
when they were human and you their child,
as though death had changed nothing.

Night Song

Among rocks, I am the loose one,
among arrows, I am the heart,
among daughters, I am the recluse,
among sons, the one who dies young.

Among answers, I am the question,
between lovers, I am the sword,
among scars, I am the fresh wound,
among confetti, the black flag.

Among shoes, I am the one with the pebble,
among days, the one that never comes,
among the bones you find on the beach,
the one that sings was mine.

The Need To Hold Still

34   Winter weeds,
survivors
of a golden age,
take over the open land,
pale armies
redressing the balance

Again we live
in a time of fasting,
burlap cassocks,
monks on their knees,
bells tolling
in an empty sky

among the thin,
the trampled on,
the inarticulate
clothed in drafts
and rooted in shocked earth
which remembers nothing

fields and fields of them

                    *

Teasel
yarrow
goldenrod
wheat
bedstraw
Queen Anne's lace
drop-seed
love grass:
plain, strong names,
bread and water

A woman
coming in from a walk
notices how drab
her hair has become
that gray and brown
are colors
she disappears into

that her body
has stopped asking
for anything except calm

                    *

When she brings them
into the house
and shortens them
for the vase,
their stems break
like old bones,
clean

No holding on
No bitter odor
No last drop of juice

Hers, as long as she wants them

Their freedom from either/or
will outlast hers every time

                    *

36 The dignity of form
after seduction
and betrayal
by color

the heads,
separate,
but held together
by an old design
no one has thought
to question

the open pods
that have given
and given again

dullness of straw,
which underlies
the rose
the grape
the kiss

the narrow leaf blades,
shape of the body

the fine stems,
earliest brush strokes,
lines in the rock
on the wall
the page

III

Voices from the Forest

1. *The Voice of the Traveler Who Escaped*

No matter how exhausted you are,
and though you think you will die of thirst,
do not enter the house in the forest.
Ignore the unlocked door
and the lamp in the window, lit for you.
Pass the house, which is real
and warm and apparently safe,
where the traveler is received
by someone, or at least
by a fire and a spread table.
It is only when you finish eating
and, drowsy and grateful, pull off your shoes,
that the ax falls or the giant returns
or the monster springs or the witch
locks the door from the outside
and throws away the key.

2. *Warning to Virgins*

Each year you become more wary,
less easily taken in,
but my disguises still fool you.
Today I will go as the bear
who lumbers to the door
of two young beauties, to be brushed
and petted, and to eat
out of their hands. Yesterday
I was the prince of frogs
hopping up golden stairs
to sheets that smelled of the sun.
Tomorrow I'll live, an unspecified beast,
in a marvelous castle, enjoying
the echo chamber, my godlike roar.
You know the girl, and how
she will discover the human.
But I'm not through; I'll come
and trick you, long-legged darling,
baby blond, with my wizened face,

40 my dwarf's cap and ridiculous voice.
Watch out for little men
at crossroads, who give you directions
and ask to share your supper:
one slip of the tongue, and you lose.
There is no second chance.

3. *A Voice from out of the Night*

Remember me, I was a celebrity,
the famous beauty. All mirrors confirmed me,
the panel of judges ogled me
and cast a unanimous vote.
I was asked my opinion
on marriage, men, abortion,
the use of liquor and drugs;
that was a long time ago.

When my voice deepened
and a bristle
appeared under my chin,
when my blond hair
developed gray roots
and my waist thickened,
the rumors started.
When my legs became sticks
and small brown toads
spotted the backs of my hands,
everyone believed them.
I was accused of devouring children
and mutilating men;
they said I smelled of old age
and strong home remedies.
They cast me into the forest
but come to me secretly, in the dark,
in their times of trouble.
What could I have done to convince them
I was not guilty?
Loss of beauty was all
the proof they needed.

Young wives in love with your men,
kissing your babies: this
could be a warning, but what is the use?
Husbands will flee you,
sons will turn on you,
daughters will throw up their hands
and cry, "Not me! Not me!"

4. *The Hunter's Voice*

Happily, I am exempt
from your bazaar of punishments
and rewards, the way you pass out beauty
and hold the burning shoes in abeyance
until the pendulum swings.
I will accept an assignment
from anyone who pays me,
and if the heart I bring back as proof
is not the intended one,
who is to know? I wear green,
not your colors of blood and snow;
I disappear among trees
and am not missed.
You would never believe
I have changed the plot of your lives.

5. *The False Bride's Side of the Story*

Kindness ran in your blood,
poverty spiked mine.

Nature gave you beauty,
mine came from tubes of paint.

You were a trusting fool,
I tried to take care of myself.

You wept genuine diamonds,
I wept plain salt tears.

You kept warm in a paper dress,
I froze in furs and woolens.

42   You found love without trying,
I took your lover but failed at love.

Your wedding ring kept shining,
mine turned black the first night.

Your baby was plump and bright-eyed,
mine was a monster disguised as a child.

Sister, my soul, my twin
on the other end of our seesaw,
any moment now
you will rise to the top, resurrected,
your cheeks swelling like plums,
while I go down to my death.
There the story breaks off
for the sake of the children who listen,
but don't be too sure. One day,
one afternoon, as you sit
(a calm Vermeer in sunlight)
counting your blessings like stitches,
I may step out of the sun,
large and dark as life.

6. *The Third Son's Confession*

Early on I was chosen
the one least likely to succeed.
I was made fun of, but got away
with daydreaming and learning the language
of wood doves and white snakes.
My brothers were ambitious
and steady; they made maps
of possible trails through the forest,
they trained for months
for the climb up the glass mountain,
they monitored their shudders
to overcome fear on the field of bones.
I wished them luck, but they failed,
they came home defeated and bitter,
and I, late bloomer intending nothing,

found myself on the other side
of the forest, across the boneyard,
on top of the glass mountain.
Don't ask me if I was chosen
or simply lucky. Years ago
I threw a penny down a well,
but I've forgotten the wish.

7. *Flesh and Blood*

This is my brother the fat, caged boy
This is my brother the spotted fawn
These are my brothers the seven ravens
These are my brothers the six mute swans

I have a plan for my brother the boy
I have a hermit's shack for my fawn
I've cut off a finger to save my ravens
I've given up speech to save my swans

Help me, whispers my brother the boy
Play with me, begs my high-stepping fawn
Why were you born, lament the ravens
You caused our exile, accuse the swans

Brothers, my brothers, I am your sister
I am a woman, I will be a wife
I am your face in the altered mirror
I will give you back your life

Brother my boy, you'll grow thin and forget me
You'll play with another, brother my fawn
Human, my seven, you will hunt ravens
Human, you'll leave me, my six mute swans

8. *The Voice from Under the Hazel Bush*

I died for you. Each spring
I wake in my house of roots;
my memory leafs out
into a rich green dress
for you to dance in. The moon

44 turns it to silver, the evening sun
    to gold. Be happy, my daughter.
    You think I have magic powers,
    others call it love.
    I tell you it is the will
    to survive, in you, in the earth.
    Your story does not end
    with the wedding dance, it goes on.

IV

The Triumph of Life: Mary Shelley

The voice addressing us is that of Mary Wollstonecraft Shelley, 1796–
1851, daughter of the radical philosopher William Godwin and the
feminist Mary Wollstonecraft, who died as a result of her birth. She
eloped with Percy Shelley, who was married to Harriet Westbrook at
the time, and became his second wife after Harriet committed suicide.
Shelley and Mary lived a nomadic life, moving around England and the
Continent, never settling down anywhere for long. Three of their four
children died in infancy. Their eight years together were a series of
crises, many of them brought about by Shelley's restlessness and the
drain of outsiders on their emotional and physical resources. After
Shelley's accidental drowning, Mary, who was twenty-four at the time
of his death, supported herself and their surviving son by her own writ-
ing and by editing and annotating Shelley's work. She published the
first complete edition of his poems. Her own works consist of essays,
short stories, and six novels, of which *Frankenstein*, written when she
was nineteen, is the most famous. Her journal has been an important
biographical source for Shelley's and her life together.

I

My father taught me to think
to value mind over body,
to refuse even the airiest cage

to be a mouth as well as an ear,
to ask difficult questions,
not to marry because I was asked,
not to believe in heaven

None of this kept me from bearing
four children and losing three
by the time I was twenty-two

He wanted to think I sprang
from his head like the Greek goddess

He forgot that my mother died
of my birth, *The Rights of Women*
washed away in puerperal blood
and that I was her daughter too

2

I met him when I was sixteen
He came to sit at my father's feet
and stayed to sit at mine

We became lovers
who remained friends
even after we married

A marriage of true minds
It is what you want
It is what we wanted

We did not believe in power
We were gentle
We shared our bodies with others
We thought we were truly free

My father taught us there was a solution
to everything, even evil

We were generous, honest
We thought we had the solution

and still, a woman walked
into the water because of us

3

After that death I stopped
believing in solutions

And when my children died
it was hard not to suspect
there was a god, a judgment

For months I wanted to be
with those three small bodies,
to be still in a dark place

No more mountain passes
No more flight from creditors
with arms as long as our bills

No more games to find out
who was the cleverest of us all
No more ghost stories by the fire
with my own ghosts at the window,
smiles sharpened like sickles
on the cold stone of the moon

For months I made a fortress
of my despair
"A defect of temper," they called it
His biographers never liked me

You would have called it a sickness,
given me capsules and doctors,
brushes and bright paints,
kits for paper flowers

4

An idea whose time has come,
you say about your freedom
but you forget the reason

Shall I remind you of history,
of choice and chance, the wish and the world,
of courage and locked doors,
biology and fate?

I wanted what you want,
what you have

If I could have chosen my children
and seen them survive
I might have believed in equality,
written your manifestos

Almost two hundred years
of medical science divide us

5

And yet, my father was right
It was the spirit that won in the end

After the sea had done
what it could to his flesh
I knew he was my husband
only by the books
in his pockets: Sophocles, Keats

The word survives the body

It was then I decided
not to marry again
but to live for the word

6

I allowed his body to be burned
on that Italian beach
Rome received his ashes

You have read that our friend
snatched his heart from the fire
You call it a grisly act,
something out of my novel

You don't speak of the heart
in your letters, your sharp-eyed poems
You speak about your bodies
as though they had no mystery,
no caves, no sudden turnings

You claim isolation, night-sweats,
hanging on by your teeth

You don't trust the heart
though you define death
as the absence of heartbeat

You would have taken a ring,
a strand of hair, a shoelace
—a symbol, a souvenir

not the center, the real thing

7

He died
and the world gave no outward sign

I started a Journal of Sorrow

But there were the words, the poems,
passion and ink spilling
over the edges of all those sheets
There was the hungry survivor
of our bodily life together

Would it have lasted, our marriage,
if he had stayed alive?

As it was, we fed each other
like a pair of thrushes
I gave his words to the world
and they came back to me
as bread and meat and apples,
art and nature, mind and flesh
keeping each other alive

His last, unfinished poem
was called *The Triumph of Life*

8

You are surprised at my vision,
that a nineteen-year-old girl
could have written that novel,
how much I must have known

But I only wanted to write
a tale to tremble by,
what is oddly called a romance

By accident I slid
out of my century
into yours of white-coated men
in underground installations,
who invent their own destruction
under fluorescent lights

52 And in a few more decades,
    when your test-tube babies sprout,
    you will call me the prophet
    of ultimate horror again

    It was only a private nightmare
    that dreamed the arrogance of your time

    I was not your Cassandra
    In any age, life has to be lived
    before we can know what it is

Children's Corner

Hopscotch

The world is a place of square cages
through which you pass into heaven.
A small stone is your guide.
You make it hard on yourself,
shackle your feet, give up a leg,
invent circuitous routes:
it may take you ages.
When you arrive nothing happens.
It is only another piece
of the scarred, gray pavement,
and you receive no reward
except the desire to try again.

Hide-and-Seek

Someone is always hiding
his face behind his hands,
pretending to see nothing

while someone else runs off
to disappear in the woods
or stand in the shadows of tall buildings
holding his breath.

London Bridge

Not only heaven, but hell is here.
Two angels, one of them fallen,
divide the world between them.

You are in the middle when it collapses.

Now you must choose your afterlife;
a choice between peaches and plums,
oil and gold, red and white stripes,
black and white tyrants, the left and right horn.
Think hard. Both angels smile.

Ghosts

You are two-thirds of a ghost,
headed for extinction,
because you did not know
words were that important.

Who am I?

The others sit in a circle.
They have names and faces,
voices you can identify.
Blank, you arrive among them,
a feedsack filled with straw,
and ask them for your life.

Pinning the Tail on the Donkey

You can't be sure where the donkey is,
or if there *is* a donkey
and you are holding a tail.
You might be pinning a beard on a baby
or a willow leaf on the moon.
You must resist such questions
and assume a tailless donkey,
patient and flat as the map of the world,
is waiting for you to make him whole.
The presumption is of a botched job,
but you come as close as you can.

The Story

You are telling a story:
How Fire Took Water to Wife

It's always like this, you say,
opposites attract

They want to enter each other,
be one,
so he burns her as hard as he can
and she tries to drown him

It's called love at first
and doesn't hurt

but after a while she weeps
and says he is killing her,
he shouts that he cannot breathe
underwater—

Make up your own
ending, you say to the children,
and they will, they will

Testimony

56   You forget I was in the sea
a long time, breathing through gills,
before I surfaced on that shell,
the "glorious moment" you speak of.
Nor did you notice my folded lungs
fight for that first deep draft of air.
Telling the story, you omit
that in the beginning my hair was green,
seaweed, before it turned
into the yellow silk you admire.
You paint me floating ashore
with rose-tipped breasts lifting
toward the sun, and the sun avid;
and you say I stepped into heated shoes
of glittering white sand.
What poor eyewitnesses you are.
I remember it was a cloudy day,
a starved dog ran along the shore,
the rocks and shells cut into my feet.
No one was there. I was cold and lost.
The scraggly leaves all pointed
in one direction, toward the interior.
I had no other place to go.

The Escape

Pain lines the inside of her skin
seamlessly, daily. She has stopped
trying to tell us how it feels,
this garment which pulls around her
closer and closer, while she shrinks
into it, trying to fit,
an insect wrapping itself
in its shift of denial.
How silent it is,
the labor of getting smaller
until so little is left of her
that she can escape through a pinhole.
She is dreaming a dream of flight,
a disappearance so perfect
that we suspect nothing:
she imagines us at her bedside,
accepting her muteness, her turned-away face
as usual, while she speeds
outward through unimagined space,
already a star without memory.

Seeing Them on Television

The miners' wives and children
come down like shepherds
from the hills,
group themselves as if in a painting

It is not that they are hungry
or clothed in rags,
but their faces are like those
of the imagined poor,
blackened by disaster
and weary from waiting
for news of a miracle

We see them flattened,
a single image,
the ancient crowd of mourners
in a continual passion play,
a tableau behind a voice
that has dropped low enough
for decorum

The Artist's Model, ca. 1912

In 1886 I came apart—

I who had been Mme. Rivière,
whole under flowing silk,
had sat on the grass, naked,
my body an unbroken invitation—

splintered into thousands
of particles, a bright rock
blasted to smithereens;
even my orange skirt dissolved
into drops that were not orange.

Now they are stacking me like a child's
red and blue building blocks,
splitting me down the middle,
blackening half my face;

they tell me the world has changed,
haven't I heard, and give me
a third eye, a rooster's beak.

I ask for my singular name
back, but they say in the future
only my parts will be known,
a gigantic pair of lips,
a nipple, slick as candy,

and that even those will disappear,
white on white or black on black,
and you will look for me
in the air, in the absence of figure,
in space, inside your head,
where I started, your own work of art.

The End of Science Fiction

This is not fantasy, this is our life.
We are the characters
who have invaded the moon,
who cannot stop their computers.
We are the gods who can unmake
the world in seven days.

Both hands are stopped at noon.
We are beginning to live forever,
in lightweight, aluminum bodies
with numbers stamped on our backs.
We dial our words like muzak.
We hear each other through water.

The genre is dead. Invent something new.
Invent a man and a woman
naked in a garden,
invent a child that will save the world,
a man who carries his father
out of a burning city.
Invent a spool of thread
that leads a hero to safety;
invent an island on which he abandons
the woman who saved his life
with no loss of sleep over his betrayal.

Invent us as we were
before our bodies glittered
and we stopped bleeding:
invent a shepherd who kills a giant,
a girl who grows into a tree,
a woman who refuses to turn
her back on the past and is changed to salt,
a boy who steals his brother's birthright
and becomes the head of a nation.

Invent real tears, hard love,
slow-spoken, ancient words,
difficult as a child's
first steps across a room.

What Will You Do

What did you do when the glacier
paved your mouth with ice
    when your scales fell off
and were left on the ground to rust
    when you stopped treading water
and started breathing air

What did you do when you realized
you were different from the others
    when you were cheated of your fur
your prehensile tail
    when death revealed itself
as the Supreme Being
unappeasable

And what did you do when the sun
stopped revolving around you
    when animals started to disappear
and the trees loosened their roots
imperceptibly at first
so you would not notice
    when water declared an eye for an eye
and pumped your poison back into you

and when your children left you
and joined the enemy
    when the air became colder and colder
and you moved faster than sound
though your love letter never got there
    what did you do when history
fell down at your feet
and asked to start all over

That's what you will do

Why We Tell Stories
For Linda Foster

I

Because we used to have leaves
and on damp days
our muscles feel a tug,
painful now, from when roots
pulled us into the ground

and because our children believe
they can fly, an instinct retained
from when the bones in our arms
were shaped like zithers and broke
neatly under their feathers

and because before we had lungs
we knew how far it was to the bottom
as we floated open-eyed
like painted scarves through the scenery
of dreams, and because we awakened

and learned to speak

2

We sat by the fire in our caves,
and because we were poor, we made up a tale
about a treasure mountain
that would open only for us

and because we were always defeated,
we invented impossible riddles
only we could solve,
monsters only we could kill,
women who could love no one else

and because we had survived
sisters and brothers, daughters and sons,
we discovered bones that rose
from the dark earth and sang
as white birds in the trees

3

Because the story of our life
becomes our life

Because each of us tells
the same story
but tells it differently

and none of us tells it
the same way twice

Because grandmothers looking like spiders
want to enchant the children
and grandfathers need to convince us
what happened happened because of them

and though we listen only
haphazardly, with one ear,
we will begin our story
with the word *and*